A Girl's World

A Girl's World

A Social Emotional Workbook for Teen Girls

Amanda Winter

ISBN: 1523375876
ISBN 13: 9781523375875

About this Workbook

I WANTED TO write a collection of group activities where individuals can engage in discussion and learn skills that will promote their social and emotional well-being. Important topics will be discussed such as self-esteem, feelings, communication, friendship, and relationships. There is also a section about technology and social media. As technology continues to advance adolescents need to be educated about how to engage in appropriate cyber behavior as well as how to protect themselves physically and emotionally.

My hope for this workbook is that individuals will be able to participate in beneficial discussions and written exercises, share personal experiences, learn skills, all while having fun. Group facilitators can pick and choose lessons that most relate to the group needs. Since it can be difficult to always find the time to implement lessons, I include lesson plans that range between 20-45 minutes.

Social Media/Technology

How Social Media Affects Me

Objective: For girls to identify how their social media communication habits are affecting their lives.

Procedure: Start a discussion about how technology is a big part of our lives and how it continues to advance. Although a lot of us use technology to make our lives easier, it can also make aspects of our lives more complicated. When used appropriately, we can use technology in a variety of ways to help us. We are able to stay connected to people we don't typically see, can set up plans easily by sending a quick text message, or research topics within a matter of seconds. Sometimes, communicating with social media can lead people to say mean things they normally wouldn't say to someone else. It's easier to type hurtful words to a computer screen or a phone screen than it is to say something hurtful to someone directly.

Distribute journaling charts to girls in the group and explain that they will be keeping track of their conversations that they have using texting, group chats, or other apps and social media sites in which they communicate regularly to their peers. Ask them to keep write in their journals for a week or until the next group session. Afterwards, the group can explore their own communication patterns while using technology to determine if the effects are more positive or negative.

PRE- DISCUSSION QUESTIONS

1. How important is technology in your life?
2. In what ways do you use technology to talk with friends?
3. What are some of the pros and cons of using technology to talk to friends?

POST-DISCUSSION QUESTIONS

1. Were your conversations on social media sites and technology mostly negative or positive? Were you surprised?
2. Did you experience any miscommunications while using technology to talk to friends?
3. Were you feelings mostly positive or negative during and after your cyber conversations? Why?
4. If many of the conversations you have involve talking badly about someone or making you feel bad, what can you do differently in the future?
5. If you had mostly positive conversations what can you do in the future if someone starts to make you uncomfortable or starts to talk badly about someone?

Date	
Type of technology/app used?	
Were negative comments made by you?	
Were negative comments made about you?	
How did you feel after the conversation?	
Date	
Type of technology/app used?	
Were negative comments made by you?	
Were negative comments made about you?	
How did you feel after the conversation?	
Date	
Type of technology/app used?	
Were negative comments made about you?	
How did you feel after the conversation?	

Date	
Type of technology/app used?	
Were negative comments made by you?	
Were negative comments made about you?	
How did you feel after the conversation?	
Date	
Type of technology/app used?	
Were negative comments made by you?	
Were negative comments made about you?	
How did you feel after the conversation?	
Date	
Type of technology/app used?	
Were negative comments made about you?	
How did you feel after the conversation?	

Don't Let Social Media Control Your Life

Objective: For girls to develop a healthy perspective about social media and how it can affect their feelings.

Information: Sometimes individuals can get too focused on social media instead of real life. We fall into traps that lead us to feel sad or hurt. Look at the following situations and write out how each example might make people feel badly. Afterwards, write out a positive thought or healthy outlook on the situation.

- You are super focused on the number of likes you get after posting a picture.

  Negative Thought/Feeling:

  Healthy Outlook:

- You notice a group of friends did something fun over the weekend, but didn't invite you.

  Negative Thought/Feeling:

  Healthy Outlook:

- It seems like someone else has the perfect life. She always looks great in pictures and is constantly surrounded by friends in her pictures.

  Negative Thought/Feeling:

  Healthy Outlook:

- You send a message to a friend, but don't receive a response back after an hour.

  Negative Thought/Feeling:

  Healthy Outlook:

- The person you like posted a picture of him/her and another student from your school with a new status: "In a relationship."

  Negative Thought/Feeling:

  Healthy Outlook:

DISCUSSION QUESTIONS

1. Which situation do you relate to the most?
2. What do you think other people your age relate to the most?
3. How can social media impact someone's self-esteem?
4. What do you think is a helpful strategy to maintain a healthy perspective on viewing other people's social media profiles?
5. What are a few things you like to do in real life that you can't replicate online?

RUDETEXTING

Object: For girls to learn boundaries regarding texting and when it's appropriate to put the phone away.

Procedure: Have group members fill out their answers and then discuss responses afterwards.

Situation: Texting at the dinner table

How does it affect others?

What could you be missing out on?

Situation: Texting while babysitting

How does it affect others?

What could you be missing out on?

Situation: Texting at your table during lunch

How does it affect others?

What could you be missing out on?

Situation: Texting while you're on a date

How does it affect others?

What could you be missing out on?

Situation: Texting during class

How does it affect others?

What could you be missing out on?

DISCUSSION QUESTIONS

1. Do you think people were better or worse at communicating 20 years ago? Why or why not?
2. What do you think will be the most common way to communicate 20 years into the future?
3. What are pros and cons to texting?
4. What are places where you find people texting the most often?
5. What are some of your ideas about how to help others reduce rude texting behaviors?

SELFIE CRAZE

Objective: For girls to develop a healthy perspective on "selfie" habits.

Procedure: Have group members fill out the following questionnaire. Afterwards, process their answers as a group and go over the discussion questions.

1. I like to take selfies because:

2. How many selfies do you take per day/week?

3. Describe the perfect "selfie."

4. How do you feel when you post a selfie and don't get a certain amount of likes?

5. How do you feel when someone else posts the "perfect selfie?"

6. When I go out to different places I never forget to take a selfie.   True/False

DISCUSSION QUESTIONS

1. Do you think you have a healthy/unhealthy selfie taking habit? Why?
2. What are your thoughts about individuals who take selfies regularly?
3. How can focusing on taking "perfect selfies" regularly have negative consequences on your self-esteem?
4. Do you think our society is moving to a selfie obsessed culture? If so, what are some implications that we might find?
5. How will you find the right balance when it comes to taking selfies and enjoying being in the moment?

Cyber Friend or Faux

Objective: For girls to learn how to recognize the difference between friends and "cyber friends."

Information: Who are cyber friends? They are people you talk to on Facebook, Instagram or other social networking sites, but haven't had the chance to meet in person.

Make sure to never accept a friend request from someone you do not know. It doesn't count if they say they know one of your friends, but you have never met them before. Safety is important! You need to know who you are talking to and unfortunately, some people may lie about their identities. Cyber friends haven't earned our trust yet. Real friendships take time to build. They are based on trust, respect, and shared interests. Most cyber friends are acquaintances as opposed to close friends. Have girls write answers to the following questions and then go over answers. Acceptable things to do or say to friends could be asking if they want to come over to hang out or you can share secret or personal information with them. Emphasize the importance in not sharing personal information with cyber friends such as addresses or locations.

Discussion Questions

1. What are acceptable things to say or do with a friend?
2. What are acceptable things to do or say with a cyber friend?
3. What are things that you should not say or share with a cyber friend?
4. How easy/difficult is it for someone to pretend to be someone they're not?

How Much is Too Much

Objective: For girls to learn to how to think before posting information on their social media profiles.

Procedure: How much information is ok for others to see? What should I keep private? Adolescents are trying to figure out their own self-image and how they fit into the world. Some individuals might use their profiles as a way to express themselves and to show others who they are and what makes them unique. However, everything that we post about ourselves online is open for everyone to see. Girls must understand that once something is posted that information is in cyberspace and open for anyone to see. There are no true privacy settings or confidentiality online so make sure you think before posting! After going over questions that girls should ask themselves before posting information, have group members fill out their profile with information that they think is safe for others to know and that they would be comfortable sharing. Also, have the group look at the worksheet with the example of a profile to go over what they think should be changed.

1. Would I feel comfortable if my parents saw my profile? Would I feel comfortable if all the kids in school saw my profile? Would I feel comfortable if my future children saw my profile?
2. How does my profile picture represent who I am? What kind of picture do I feel comfortable posting?
3. What kind of profile pictures would be inappropriate to post?
4. Should I post a status about my location? Is that safe? Are there people who I wouldn't feel comfortable knowing where I am?
5. Should I post a negative comment about someone else? What are the consequences? Am I really angry? Would I regret this later?
6. Do I want other people to know my email address or phone number?
7. What are some negative consequences that could result from posting information about you that is not true? Ex. You pretend to be older than your actual age.

ABBY'S PROFILE

Name: Abby Nicole Smith

Address: 5252 Maple Avenue, Chicago, IL 60605

Phone Number: (555) 299-0478

Email Address: sweetiepie22@gmail.com

Birthday: June 1st

School: Forest Trails

Relationship status: Single

Interests: Hanging with friends, going to concerts, playing soccer, PARTYING!!

Favorite Bands: Too many to name!

Status: So sick of people thinking they're so cool when really no one actually likes them! *With Katie Johnson and Taylor Fischer.*

My Profile

Name:
Address:
Phone Number:
Email Address:
Birthday:
School:
Relationship status:
Interests:
Favorite Bands:
Status:

To Send or Not To Send

—✦—

Objective: For girls to realize the possibly harmful consequences of sending a sexy picture or "sexting" someone.

Once you send a picture of yourself to someone you have no power over where it ends up. Once something is posted on the internet it will be somewhere in cyber- space indefinitely.

1. What are things that friends share with each other online?

2. What are some reasons why people send nude pictures or "sexy pictures" of themselves to others?

3. Why do some people have trouble saying "No" if asked for nude pictures?

4. What are different ways to say, "No?" Practice different ways and pick one that makes you comfortable.

5. How would you feel if everyone at school saw your pictures?

6. Could people get in trouble for sending nude pictures or resending nude pictures?

7. What does it mean to have respect for yourself?

8. How can taking nude photos of yourself and keeping them on your phone or computer still be a risky move?

9. What advice would you give to a friend who is debating on whether or not she should send someone a nude picture?

10. What is something you can say to yourself to remind you of the consequences that could happen if you send a nude picture?

CYBER SAFETY QUIZ

Objective: For girls to test their cyber safety knowledge.

Procedure: Have girls take the quiz. Once everyone is finished go over their answers and see if they match the correct responses. Engage in a discussion about their responses.

1. I should make a password that is simple so I can remember it easily.

    TRUE   **FALSE**

2. I should never share my address or phone number on a social media site.

    TRUE   **FALSE**

3. I can accept a friend request from someone I don't know as long as they're my age.

    TRUE   **FALSE**

4. The more friends I have online the better.

    TRUE   **FALSE**

5. It's important not to share my location when taking pictures on Instagram.

    TRUE   **FALSE**

6. I am responsible enough to use a credit card online to buy something that I want.

    TRUE   **FALSE**

7. It's better to work out an argument with a friend through text messaging than in person.

    TRUE   **FALSE**

8. Meeting new friends online is a great way to meet new people.

    TRUE   **FALSE**

9. If someone sends me an inappropriate message it's best to not let an adult   know about it.

    TRUE   **FALSE**

10. Creating a fake profile with false information is fun and nothing bad can   come out of it.

    TRUE   **FALSE**

List personal information that would not be appropriate to share on a social media site.

1.
2.
3.

ANSWER KEY:

1. **False:** It's important to make a password that others won't be able to guess. Doing so will help protect your account against hackers. For example, don't use your pet's name or birthdate because it would be too easy for others to guess that if they attempt to hack your account.

2. **True:** Never share personal information on a social media site such as phone number, address, or school. That information should only be shared with close friends and family that you trust.

3. **False:** Unfortunately, there are many sneaky adults that pretend to be teenagers. This can lead to dangerous situations. Never accept a friend request from anyone you don't know!

4. **False:** It might seem like a popularity contest at times about who can have the most friends or followers, but it's better to have a small group of friends that you trust than a large group of acquaintances.

5. **True**: Make sure to take that setting off your Instagram account. Even if you only have trusted friends who follow you there's always a possibility that someone you don't trust might find out where you are at any given moment if you are constantly posting pictures.

6. **True and False:** This is a decision that you will have to make with your parents. Be careful about using your credit card online because some sites are trusted sites and others are not.

7. **False:** Although it's uncomfortable, it's usually best to work out an argument in person. Things can be miscommunicated easily through text messages and people might text mean things without thinking. When you are face to face with someone it forces you to think about how your words will affect their feelings. Try to find the right time and place where everyone will feel comfortable and calm.

8. **False:** Although it is possible to make friends online it can be difficult to tell if a person is telling the truth about their identity. Communicating online can be a way to develop a closer friendship with someone you already know, but it's usually not a good idea to use the internet to make friends. Never invite someone over to your house if you have never met them before. If you believe you made a friend online and want to meet only do so with your parent's permission and make sure it's in a public place with other friends around.

9. **False:** Let a trusted adult know if you receive an inappropriate message from someone. They will help guide you with how to handle it.

10. **False:** You shouldn't create fake profiles even if it's just a joke. You're lying about your identify which could lead to dangerous situations.

Tech Savvy

Objective: For girls to discuss the positive and negative uses of different apps. This information should also be shared with parents. It is important to encourage girls and adolescents and their parents to have frequent open discussions about social media usage.

ASK FM Ask.fm is a site where individuals can post a question or post an answer to a question. Users can select whether or not they want to keep their posts anonymous or they can use their name. Be aware that due to the anonymity of posts, there have been many cases of cyberbullying where users can post unkind comments about someone that can be viewed by the Ask.fm community. Age requirements state that users must be 13 years old use Ask.fm.

Snapchat- Snapchat is an app where individuals can send each other pictures, texts, or videos that will disappear after a set amount of time. The sender can select how long they want the recipient to view the message. Be aware that teenagers can use this for sending inappropriate nude pictures with the misconception that it will disappear after a few seconds. However, recipients can find ways to screenshot the image or take a picture of the screen with another device.

Whisper- Individuals who use this app can post comments on boards anonymously. There is an option to send responses publicly or privately to the users. Be aware that individuals feel protected by the anonymity factor and can post threats or information that can have negative consequences. Educate your teen about what appropriate and inappropriate content would be.

Instagram- This app allows users to post pictures with editing features such as filters for different lighting effects. Posted pictures will be viewed by the public unless the user sets a privacy setting for other users to ask permission to follow their pictures and posts. Be aware that there is an option to tag a location of your pictures that have been recently posted. Educate your teen about only accepting follow requests from people they know and that there is a possible safety concern if any user can see where they are at any moment if they are tagging their locations.

Omegle- This is a site where users are randomly matched with other users to have conversations. The site keeps users' information anonymous and leaves it up to users to share that information. Be aware that there is a possibility that conversations can involve inappropriate topics. This is an app for adults only!

Tinder- This app allows users to see other users' profiles according to desired location. A common purpose of this app is to match individuals who are interested in dating or communicating with one another. Users view other profiles and swipe one way if they are not interested in communicating with a user and swipe another direction if they are interested. Be aware that this site could affect self-esteem. Many swipes are determined whether or not a user finds the person to be attractive or not. Make sure to educate your teen about general safety information about sharing personal information with others.

Discussion Question for Group Members and Parents

1. What apps or types of social media do you use?
2. What is the purpose? Ex. Making plans with friends
3. What safety precautions are you using?
4. What plan should we put in place to make sure that you are safe?
5. Have you witnessed any rude or hurtful behavior online?
6. If you do witness rude or hurtful behaviors what will you do?
7. Are you spending enough time with friends in person?

Communication

The Right Time and Place

Objective: Teach girls the importance in choosing the right time and place when interacting with others.

Information: Social skills are an important part in developing relationships with other individuals. We pay a lot of attention to what we say and how to say it in order to make the people we are interacting with feel respected. However, it is also important to identify a good time to have certain conversation with others as well as the right place. For example, it would be appropriate to ask your friend for some help with your math homework, but not 5 minutes before she has to give a presentation in front of the whole class! Or, it would be ok if you wanted to share a secret with a friend, but not at the lunch table when other people are around.

Look at the following scenarios and decide appropriate and inappropriate times and locations to have these conversations. When would these conversations be best: In person? Online? One on one? In front of other people?

1. You want to talk to a classmate to set the record straight about a rumor you heard.
2. You want to tell a teacher that a classmate has been cheating on tests.
3. You want to work out an argument with your friend.
4. You want to invite one of your friends to a sleepover at your house this weekend.
5. You are in charge of setting up the school dance and you want to get students' feedback about what they want.
6. You want to ask your teacher for extra math help.
7. You want to tell your crush that you like him.
8. You want to ask your parents for a raise in your allowance?
9. You want to tell your teacher that a classmate is being bullied.
10. You want to check with your friend to see what time she wants to go to the basketball game tonight.

Discussion Questions

1. Can you think of a time where you chose the wrong time to handle a conflict? What happened?
2. What are some conversations that should be communicated in person as opposed to online? Why?
3. Give an example of how handling a conflict with a friend in front of other peers can make the situation worse?
4. What kind of conversations are ok to have online as opposed to in person?
5. What kind of conversations should take place in a one on one setting without any other people around?

Conflict Resolution

Objective: Help girls learn how to work out conflicts with peers.

Procedure: The following set of questions can be used to address a current conflict that is taking place or it can be used to process and reflect on past conflicts that have taken place. Girls might not understand how they play a role in either hurting or helping the situation. Sometimes people make mistakes or miscommunicate, but it's important to think about how we are communicating to best help our friendships.

Questions to Process Conflict

1. Describe the situation that caused a conflict?

2. Why do you think this happened?

3. Did someone say something out of anger?

4. Was there a miscommunication?

5. Has a similar situation happened to you before?

6. Did someone say something that should have been phrased differently?

7. What role did you have in this situation?

8. Did you make the situation better or worse? Sometimes both people involved in the conflict say something that made the situation worse.

9. What is the goal that is desired? How will this be achieved?
   - Do you want to be friends?
   - Peaceful acquaintances?
   - Co-exist separately?

10. What will you do differently the next time to make sure the same conflict doesn't occur again?

Assertive Communication

Objective: To encourage girls to use assertive communication skills.

Information: It can be uncomfortable for many individuals to engage in confrontation. Instead, many people will chose to avoid it altogether. It might be a good strategy to let some things go, but it becomes a problem when a negative situation is happening regularly. If you feel like someone is taking advantage of you or not taking your feelings into account, it is necessary to communicate assertively to get your message across. Discuss the following situations and how you can use your I Statements to let someone know how you are feeling and what you would like to see changed. Afterwards, have the group members take turns acting out the different roles in each example. The girls who are not acting will give feedback on how assertive the message was communicated.

Example: Your friend missed your birthday celebration to go out on a date with someone she likes.

I feel: hurt
When: you don't show up to an event that is so important to me
Because: you are one of my closest friends and I want to spend time with you on my birthday.

1. Your friend always insists on making the decisions about what you will do on the weekends.

   I feel_____
   when_____
   because_____.

2. An older student is always teasing you in front of other students.

   I feel_____
   when_____
   because_____.

3. 3. Your mom hasn't been to one of your basketball games yet and you have been working so hard at your practices.

   I feel_____
   when_____
   because_____.

4. Your friend has been flaking out on you a lot. She has cancelled your plans at the last minute three times in the last month.

   I feel_____
   when_____
   because_____.

5. You have two best friends, but lately you have been feeling left out. Last weekend they didn't invite you to go see a movie with them.

   I feel_____
   when_____
   because_____.

Passive Communication- Did they speak too softly? Did they not look the person in the eyes? Were they standing too far away from the person?

Assertive Communication- Did they speak at a good volume? Did they give good eye contact? Did they correctly use the "I statements?" Were they a good distance away from the person when they delivered their message?

Aggressive Communication- Did they speak too loud where it sounded like they were yelling? Was their tone of voice sarcastic? Were they standing too close to the person? Did they sound like they were blaming the other person instead of expressing how they felt?

Rumors Quiz

Objective: For girls to learn to take a proactive approach to stopping rumors.

Procedure: Have girls take the quiz about rumors. Afterwards, go over the answers with them and have a discussion about their own experiences.

1. Rumors are when people spread stories or information about someone that are probably not true.
   True/False

2. Most rumors are started by someone who wants to hurt another individual's reputation.
   True/False

3. The person who starts a rumor is the only one to blame.
   True/False

4. Once a rumor starts there is nothing anyone can do to stop it.
   True/False

5. It is best to stay away from the girl who the rumor is about because she probably wants some space.
   True/False

Answers

1. **True:** Rumors can be about information that may or may not be true.

2. **False:** A lot of times rumors start with a miscommunication. Just like when you play the game. "Telephone," the story keeps changing and changing the more people are passing along the story.

3. **False**: Even if you didn't start the rumor you're allowing it to grow by continuing to talk about it or share it with different people. The best thing to do is to act uninterested when someone shares a gossipy rumor with you. Or you can change the subject.

4. **False**: Everyone can play a part in preventing rumors from spreading. Ask yourself, "Is this something I would want people sharing about me?" If not, tell the person you're not into gossip and talk about something else.

5. **False**: When a rumor is going around about someone they might be feeling sad, lonely, or angry. It's best to continue to show support to your friend by being there for her. You can help by setting the record straight if someone asks you about the rumor. Or you can help by encouraging them to talk to a trusted adult. Respect her wishes if she doesn't want to talk about the rumor as well.

Discussion Questions

1. Have you ever had a rumor spread about you?
2. How did it make you feel? If it hasn't happened to you, how do you think it would feel?
3. Have you ever started a rumor?
4. Have you ever contributed to the spreading of a rumor?
5. What do you think are some reasons why rumors get started?
6. How do rumors contribute to people having a negative school experience?
7. What will you do in the future to prevent rumors from getting out of control?

Rumors and Gossip

Objective: For girls to learn what information should be shared with others and what information would be considered hurtful gossip or rumors.

Procedure: Read the following story about Socrates and his beliefs. Afterwards, have the girls fill out their responses to demonstrate if they understand the triple filter test. End the group by going over the discussion questions.

In ancient Greece (469 - 399 BC), Socrates was widely lauded for his wisdom.

One day an acquaintance ran up to him excitedly and said, "Socrates, do you know what I just heard about Diogenes?"

"Wait a moment," Socrates replied, "Before you tell me I'd like you to pass a little test. It's called the Triple Filter Test."

'Triple filter?" asked the acquaintance.

"That's right," Socrates continued, "Before you talk to me about Diogenes let's take a moment to filter what you're going to say. The first filter is Truth. Have you made absolutely sure that what you are about to tell me is true?"

"No," the man said, "Actually I just heard about it."

"All right," said Socrates, "So you don't really know if it's true or not. Now let's try the second filter, the filter of Goodness. Is what you are about to tell me about Diogenes something good?"

"No, on the contrary..."

"So," Socrates continued, "You want to tell me something about Diogenes that may be bad, even though you're not certain it's true?"

The man shrugged, a little embarrassed. Socrates continued, "You may still pass the test though, because there is a third filter, the filter of Usefulness. Is what you want to tell me about Diogenes going to be useful to me?"

"No, not really."

"Well," concluded Socrates, "If what you want to tell me is neither True nor Good nor even useful, why tell it to me or anyone at all?"

MAKE SURE YOU PASS THE TRIPLE FILTER TEST!

1. Is it true? Are you sure?
2. Is it something good?
3. Is it useful to me?

What are four examples that would be ok to share because they pass the three rules?

1.

2.

3.

4.

What are three examples of things I would not share because they do not pass the three rules?

1.

2.

3.

4.

DISCUSSION QUESTIONS

1. What is Socrates's message in this story?
2. How does this story relate to life in current times?
3. Do people have a tough time honoring these three rules when sharing information with others? Why or why not?
4. After hearing this story what changes will you make when it comes to deciding what to share with others?
5. How do rumors and the spreading of gossip affect how people feel?

Listening Game

Objective: Group members will get to know each other while testing their listening skills.

Procedure: Every girl will take a turn sharing information about a topic of her choice for a 1 or 2 minute period while the rest of the group attempts to listen to as much information as possible. When time is up the group members will take turns recalling information that the speaker shared one person at a time.

Suggestions for Topics to Share

- Favorite vacation
- Your dream job
- Favorite school memory
- Describe your family
- Scariest dream you ever had
- Your most embarrassing moment
- If you could spend one day with anyone who would it be and what would you do?
- If you became president what would be your first order of business?
- What kind of house do you want to live in when you're older?
- Describe one of your family traditions
- What superpower would you choose to have and how would you use it?

Feelings

CHOOSE A POSITIVE ATTITUDE

Objective: To help girls understand the importance in adopting a positive attitude.

Information: There are many factors in life that we cannot control. At times negative events may occur. There will be times when you fail a test or will be turned down for a date. However, engaging in positive self-talk will help to improve our feelings and overall outlook on life. Positive attitudes are also magnetic. Individuals want to be around others who see the positive side of things People typically do not want to spend time with a person who is always negative or sees the glass as half empty because it becomes exhausting.

Choosing a positive attitude> Cause other people to choose a positive attitude too> Other people want to hang out with you>Contributes to your positive mood

Procedure: After speaking to the group about the importance in developing positive thinking patterns, face the cards down on the table. Make sure the cards are face down. Have the girls take turns picking a card. When she flips it over she will read it out loud and then state how she can turn the negative statement into a positive statement. For example, if the card read, "Nobody called me this weekend to hang out because I have no friends" it could be turned into a positive statement. The new statement could be "I didn't get to see my friend this weekend so I'll make sure to make to call them this week so we can do something fun on the weekend." After the activity have each girl brainstorm a situation where she found herself thinking negatively. Have her share the negative attitude or thought she had and how she could have changed her outlook to be more positive.

You just failed a science test.	You didn't make the basketball team.
Your friend didn't sit with you at lunch today like she normally does.	You just found out that your crush doesn't like you back.
You want to hang out at a friend's, but your mom said you have to stay home to clean your room.	You have a lot of homework to do after school today! You have to finish writing an essay, study for your science test, and do 3 pages of math.
Math is so hard! No matter how much you study the highest grade you ever earn is a "C."	You are excited to go to the amusement park with friends. When you wake up on the day of there are terrible storms going on.

Power of Positive Thinking

—⌒—

Objective: Teach girls how to challenge automatic negative thoughts and develop positive thinking patterns.

Activity- Change each negative thought into a positive thought

1. I'm never going to pass math. It's too hard and I just don't get it.
    Positive:_____
    _____
    _____

2. I'm the only girl in my school without a boyfriend.
    Positive:_____
    _____
    _____

3. I'm never going to be as good at basketball as my older sister.
    Positive:_____
    _____
    _____

4. I'm going to mess up my speech for class. I'm going to forget what to say.
    Positive:_____
    _____
    _____

5. I wasn't invited to that party over the weekend because I'm such a loser.
    Positive:_____
    _____
    _____

6. Why are my parents always on my case?!
    Positive:_____
    _____
    _____

7. My friends never invite me over to hang out on the weekends.
   Positive:_____

   _____

   _____

8. I'm going to get last place in my race at the track meet this Saturday.
   Positive:_____

   _____

   _____

9. I have to go to summer school! I won't have any time to be with my friends.
   Positive:_____

   _____

   _____

10. I just don't fit in with the people at my school.
    Positive:_____

    _____

    _____

HANDLING FEELINGS OF ANGER

Objective- For girls to determine the differences between appropriately expressing anger and behaviors that are considered mean or rude.

Procedure: Have girls come up with 7 examples for each category. A few can be used from the bank below, but they will also have to come up with examples on their own. They can work individually or with a partner. Encourage group members to think about the consequences when they decide on an appropriate way to express anger and what is considered mean or rude.

When I am angry it's ok to....

1.
2.
3.
4.
5.
6.
7.

When I am angry I won't do these behaviors because they are considered mean or rude....

1.
2.
3.
4.
5.
6.
7.

Yell at someone *Acknowledge that you're angry*
Talk about someone behind their back
Accuse someone of something without checking the facts
Confront someone in a respectful way *Vent to a friend*
Take a break Take deep breaths
Post an angry message on social media

What are coping skills I can use when I am feeling angry

1.
2.
3.
4.
5.
6.
7.
8.
9.
10.

Discussion Questions

1. How do you initially respond to anger?
2. What questions should you ask yourself to determine if it is ok to express anger in a certain way?
3. Share an example of a time when you expressed anger in an appropriate way. How about an inappropriate way?
4. How could ignoring your anger be harmful?
5. What is a new strategy that you'll try to use to cope with your anger after hearing from the other group members?

FAMILY DISCORD

Objective: For girls to process feelings about growing up where there are constant stressors.

Procedure: Girls can pick a personal issue to write out the following prompts. Afterwards, the group can go through the discussion questions.

Divorce, Alcoholism, Arguing, Yelling, Financial issues, Lack of communication, Clashing cultures, Death, Parent's loss of job,

I cannot control…
I can control…

I must accept…
This makes me feel…

I cannot control…
I can control…

I must accept…
This makes me feel…

1. Describe a situation that you would like to see changed with your family?
2. What is an important lesson you have learned from your family?
3. Name a strength you have developed from growing up in your family?
4. What skill would you like to work on to help deal with your family issues?
5. What is your favorite thing about your family?

FRIENDSHIP

Make New Friends

Objective: Teaching girls the important steps in making friends.

Procedure: Discuss "Guide to Making Friends" with your group. Be sure to encourage the girls to ask questions and share their thoughts and experiences. Afterwards, go over discussion questions as a group.

Guide to Making Friends

1. Pick a person you are interested in getting to know better. It could be someone from school, classes, clubs, sports teams, or a volunteering organization.

2. Ask them questions to get to know them better. Do they respond and ask you questions? If so, it sounds like they might be interested in getting to know you too! If the person doesn't appear interested in having a conversation with you, pick another person to get to know!

3. You don't just ask someone to be your friend. It happens naturally.   After you have had a few conversations with the person determine:
   - Does this person have similar interests as me?
   - Does this person have similar values?
   - Does this person have characteristics that I think are important in a friend?

4. Make plans to spend time with that person. If one of your shared interests is music ask if they are interested in going to a concert together.

5. Follow through with your plans! Life can get busy, but make sure to try to make time for your new friend because strong friendships occur when people get to know each other well and spend a good amount of time together.

Discussion Questions

1. What do you think are some obstacles when it comes to making friends?
2. Share one of you experiences of how you made a friend?
3. What are some feelings you have when you talk to a person for the first time?
4. Can two people be friends if they have different interests? Explain.
5. How can you tell if a person has the characteristics you are looking for in a friend?

Keeping Friends

1. Make time for your friend. Hang out on the weekends. Do fun activities together. Eat together at lunch at school.

2. Respect that they have other friends. It's great to have a lot of friends and although you might feel jealous at times, it's important to understand that your friend has other people in their lives who are important too.

3. If you are feeling left out or hurt, make sure to speak up and talk to your friend about the issue. Holding it in will only cause you to hold a grudge and could make the situation worse. When talking to your friend focus on how you feel instead of what they are doing wrong. Remember to use your "I statements!"

4. Focus on your friend. Sometimes we get wrapped up into what is going on with ourselves. Make sure that you show interest in what's going on in your friend's life. Make an effort to show you support them. For example, if being on the basketball team is really important to your friend make sure to attend a game to cheer them on!

5. Forgive your friends. Everyone makes mistakes. Sometimes we do or say things that we don't really mean. As long as the person apologizes and makes an effort to correct what they did wrong, it's good to forgive and move on!

Discussion Questions

1. What are some obstacles that come up when it comes to keeping friends?
2. Why do you think some friends drift apart? Is this always a bad thing? Why/why not?
3. What are fun things that you like to do with your friends?
4. Share an example of how you and a friend overcame an argument.

New Girl at School

Objective: To help girls develop empathy.

Procedure: Adolescents can be hypersensitive about how their peers view them. This exercise helps girls take on someone else's perspective and develop empathy for others. Have a discussion using the following questions to go over what it would be like to be the new girl at school.

1. Have you ever been the new girl at school?

2. How do you think it feels to be a new student at school?

3. What worries might be going through their minds?

4. What questions would a new student have on their first day of school?

5. What would be the worst case scenario of how someone's first day of school?

6. What would be the best case scenario of how someone's first day would go?

7. What role can you take to make sure the new student feels comfortable on her first day of school?

8. Name a few behaviors that would make a new student feel unwelcome at school?

9. Name a few behaviors that would make a student feel welcome?

10. What advice would you give the new student at your school?

11. What would you do if you overheard someone making fun of the new student?

12. How could you demonstrate leadership when it comes to talking to the new student?

Social Cue Detective

Objective: Teach girls how to pick up on social cues through the body language and tone of voice that they are using. In order to help girls maintain positive relationships with the peers and adults in their lives it's important that they are able to pick up on social cues in order to respond appropriately. Adolescents who struggle to pick up on these cues tend to struggle with finding a steady group of friends. The following scenarios will help illustrate how individuals should control their own body language and tone of voice while interpreting the social cues of others.

Procedure- Go over the following scenarios with the group. Once each question is answered and a discussion takes place, have group members act out the scenarios to demonstrate their understanding

1. What are different ways you can tell that someone is mad by viewing their body language?
2. Demonstrate what someone might sound like or do if they are not really interested in talking about video games.
3. Pretend you asked someone to hang out this weekend? Act out what the person might say or do if they weren't really interested in hanging out with you. Act out what the person might say or do if they were actually interested in hanging out with you.
4. When was the last time someone used sarcasm around you? How was it received by other people?
5. Pretend you are talking with a friend. Say the phrase "You have no idea" in two different ways. Say it the first time in a way that would be well received by the other person. The second time say it in a way that would come across as rude.
6. You told a joke to a new friend. What behaviors or actions would show that he liked your joke? What behaviors or actions would show that he did not find it funny or thought your joke was rude?
7. Your teacher just handed back the tests that the class took last week. You are proud of yourself because you got an "A." You look over to your friend and notice that he has his head down and quickly puts his test in his binder. Is this a good time to ask your friend how he did on his test? Why or why not?
8. Two boys are in the hallway pushing one another? How can you tell if this is a case of horseplay or if a fight will break out?
9. You are so bored in class! You want your teacher to see that you are paying attention and making an effort to participate. What should your body look like?
10. Your friend usually comes to sit by you in the mornings. She doesn't today though. You see her talking to another friend and assume that she is mad at you. Is this necessarily the case? What could be other reasons for what is going on?

DATING

Objective: For girls to learn to identify the differences and similarities in dating as they get older.

Information: Although many answers might differ according to the age level, it's important that girls identify what makes a relationship positive so they understand what they deserve in a relationship.

What does a date look like in middle school?

_____

_____

What qualities are important in a significant other?

_____

_____

What are signs that the relationship is good?

_____

_____

What are warning signs that the relationship is bad?

_____

_____

What does a date look like in high school?

_____

_____

What qualities are important in a significant other?

_____

_____

What are signs that the relationship is good?

_____

_____

What are warning signs that the relationship is bad?

_____

_____

What does a date look like for adults?

_____

_____

What qualities are important in a significant other?

_____

_____

What are signs that the relationship is good?

_____

_____

What are warning signs that the relationship is bad?

_____

_____

RELATIONSHIP BALANCE

Objective: For girls to understand the importance in having a healthy balance when in a relationship.

Information: It can be exciting to be in a new relationship. You might want to spend every free moment you have with that person, but it's important not to neglect the other important people and parts of your life.

Friends   Sports   Chores   Volunteer Work

Family   School   Goals   Hobbies   Me

What's Your Plan? How will you manage your time?

Time	Sun	Mon	Tues	Wed	Thurs	Fri	Sat

Fairytale Romance vs. Real Life Romance

Objective: For girls to identify the difference between fairy tale romances and real life relationships.

Information: The movies we watch and media can shape our views or expectations about what a relationship should look like. Read over the differences between a fairytale romance and a real life romance and then answer the discussion questions?

Fairytale

When you meet that special person magically fall into place

The two of you will never have a and your love will always agree.

Whenever you are facing a challenge Prince Charming will come to the rescue.

If you're upset with your prince, sing a song And you will magically feel better.

Make sure to always wear beautiful gowns and sport long wavy locks.

Real Life

Relationships take time to build. It takes a everything will while to really get to know someone.
You eventually find out what you have in common and if you're a good fit for each other.

Wrong!! You're not the same people so disagreement! You naturally you're not going to agree on everything. Make sure you respect each others' opinions and listen to one another.

It's important that both people in a relationship support one another.
However, it's vital to build independence too.
Strong problem solving skills are an important part of life.

In most cases a song won't cut it! It's important to communicate your wants and needs with your significant other.
You can't assume that they can read your mind or know what you want. Remember to use your I statements!

Whether you like to wear dresses, punk shirts, or a potato sack, the person you are dating should appreciate your unique style   and how it reflects you as a person.

Discussion Questions

1. Which fairytale description do you think most people believe? Why?
2. What types of movies do you think send fairytale messages about relationships?
3. What is another misconception that people might have about relationship expectations?
4. How can believing some of these fairytale beliefs negatively affect a relationship?
5. What do you think is the best part of being in a relationship?
6. What do you think is the most challenging part of being in a relationship?
7. What are some ways to show respect to your significant other?
8. What are qualities that make a relationship healthy?
9. How do you know if you're ready to be in a relationship?
10. Who do you know that you think has a perfect relationship? What are the qualities that make it positive?

Getting to Know Each Other Dice

Objective: For group members to get to know each other.

Activity: This activity is recommended to do during the first or second session as a way to break the ice and allow group members to become comfortable with one another. Cut out the dice and tape together. Have group members take turns rolling the dice and answer questions according to the number that they rolled. Group members can substitute in their own questions.

1. Name one thing you want to accomplish in the future.
2. Explain how your parents picked out your name when you were born.
3. What are your favorite sports to play or hobbies?
4. If you could have 3 wishes what would they be?
5. If you were an animal what would you be and why?
6. What song would you pick to represent the theme song of your life?
7. Share a fun fact about yourself.
8. If you could live anywhere in the world where would it be and why?
9. Would you describe yourself as an introvert or an extrovert?
10. What is your favorite season?
11. Share a nickname that a family member or friends has given you.
12. Who is one of your role models?

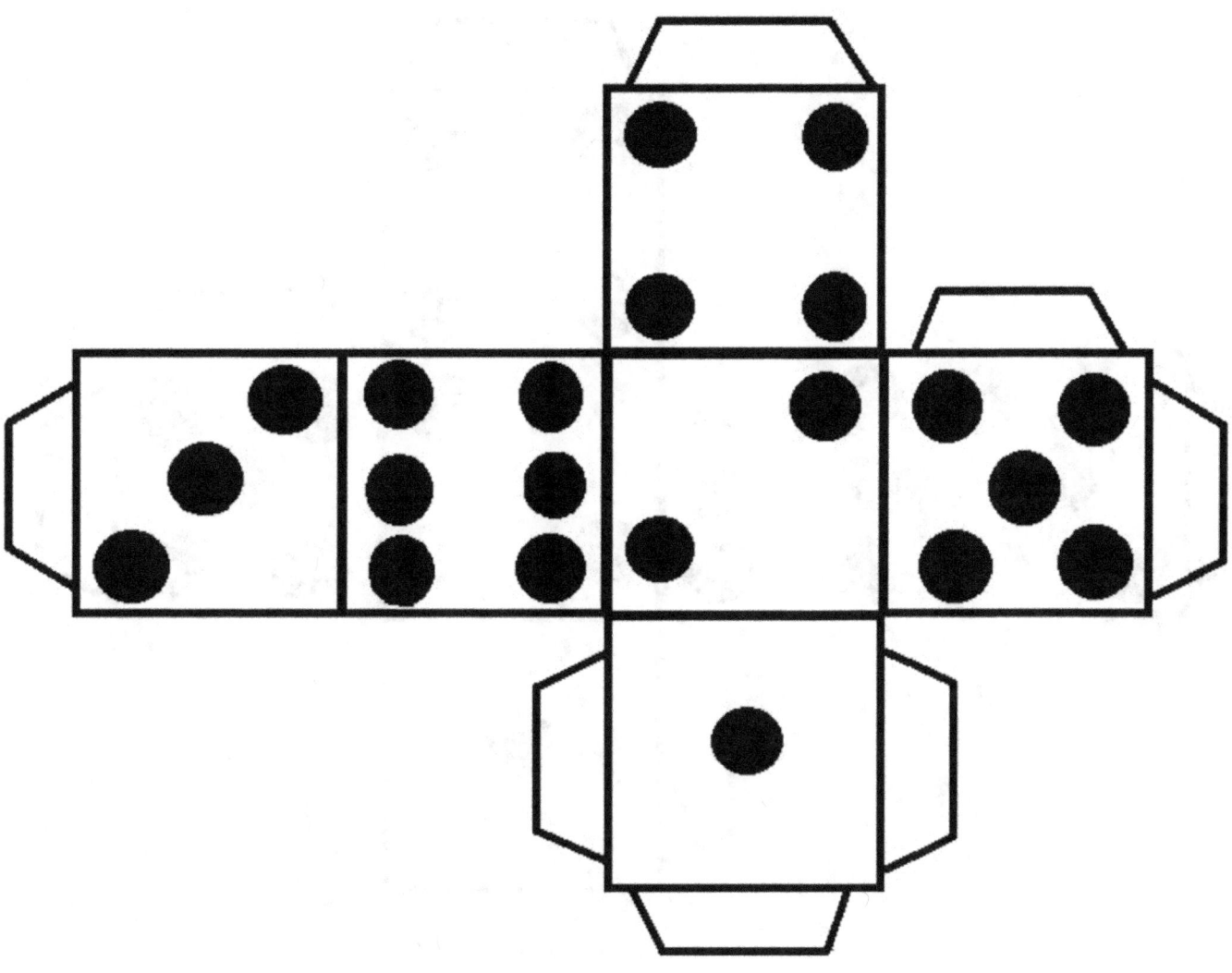

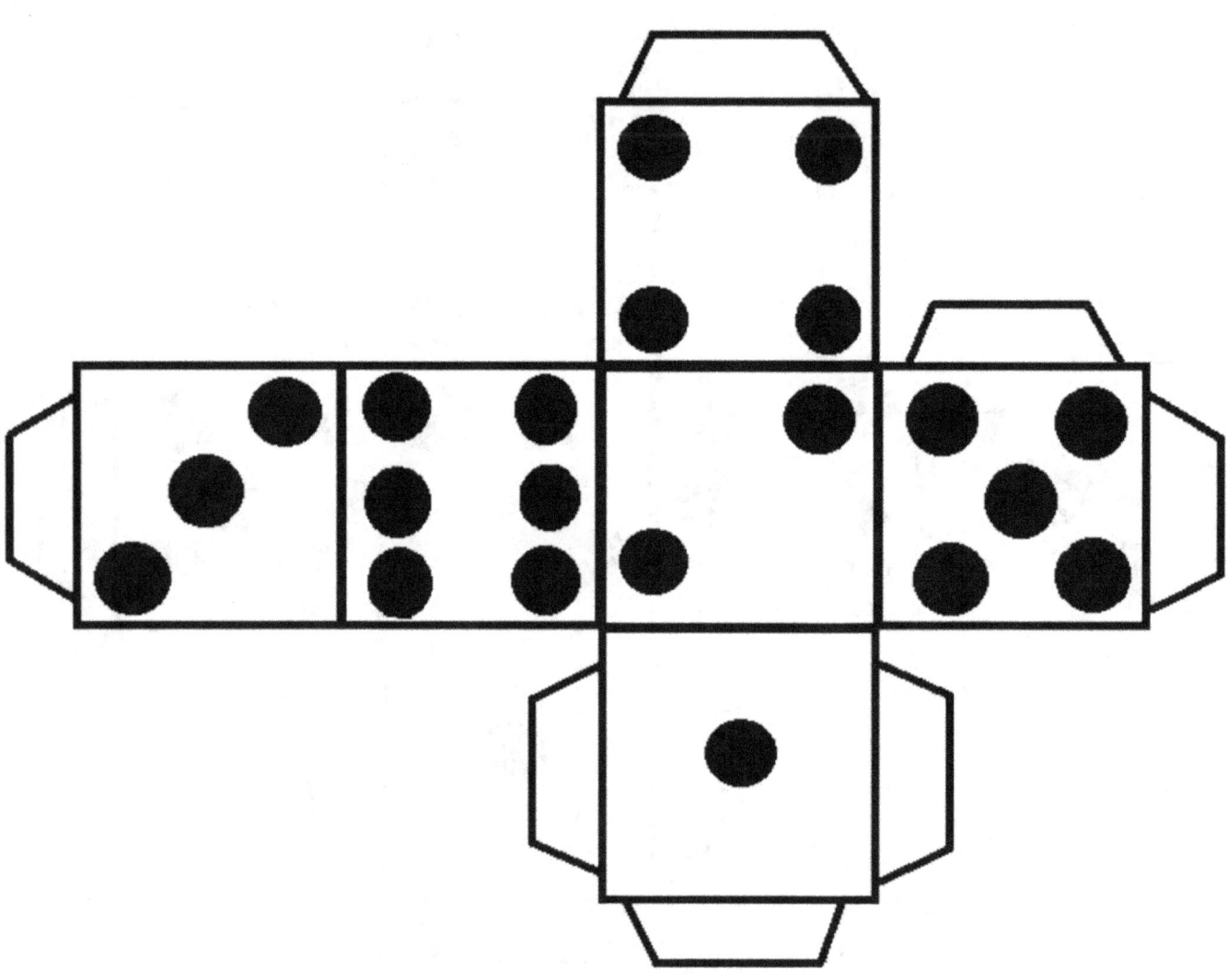

Would You Rather?

—⁓—

Objective: For girls to get to know each other by asking each other "would you rather" questions.

1. Would you rather live by the beach or in the mountains?
2. Would you rather eat pizza or burgers if you could only eat one food for the rest of your life?
3. Would you rather go on a road trip in the U.S.A. or travel to Europe?
4. Would you rather be a ballerina or a soccer player?
5. Would you rather be a talker or a listener?
6. Would you rather be able to fly or to read minds?
7. Would you rather not be able to talk for a day or not be able to hear?
8. Would you rather live in a tree house in the jungle or in an igloo?
9. Would you rather have 10 "ok" friends or 1 best friend?
10. Would you rather live in a big city or out in the country?
11. Would you rather read a book or watch a movie?
12. Would you rather go scuba diving or skydiving?
13. Would you rather have a dog or a cat as a pet?
14. Would you rather be an only child or have 6 siblings?
15. Would you rather take a test or give a presentation in front of your classmates?
16. Would you rather be known as being "popular" or "kind?"
17. Would you rather eat sweet or salty food?
18. Would you rather go to a concert or to a baseball game?
19. Would you rather travel back in time or travel to the future?
20. Would you rather be an artist or a professional athlete?
21. Would you rather visit the Grand Canyon or the Great Wall of China?
22. Would you rather travel the world for a year or donate a large amount of money to a charity?
23. Would you rather spend the day at an amusement park or at a museum?
24. Would you rather give or receive a present?
25. Would you rather spend a week without your phone or a t.v.?

STRESS MANAGEMENT

VISUALIZATION

Object: To teach girls a visualization activity to practice mindfulness.

Information: Mindfulness is a useful technique used in order to teach individuals how to focus on the present as a way to cope with stress and anxiety. Instead of worrying about the future or feeling bad about events in the past, mindfulness allows us to focus on our surroundings and how our body responds to our environment.

Draw a picture of your "happy place." Is it in the comfort of your bedroom or on a tropical island? Make sure to include as much detail as possible. Have group members write a paragraph to describe their "happy place." Use the following questions as a guide to completing the visual.

1. What does it smell like there?
2. What does it feel like there?
3. What do you hear there?
4. What does it look like there?
5. Can you taste anything?

Encourage girls to keep their visuals with them as a tool to use for relaxation.

Example: My happy place is on the beach. There are a few palm trees in the sand and the sun is nice and bright high in the sky. The water is turquoise and you can see the fish swimming around if you look down. The sand is white and powdery. I have a blue towel that is spread out on the powder sand and a multi-colored umbrella to give me some shade if needed. I feel calm and relaxed when I am at my happy place. The sand feels soft and soothes the bottom of my feet as I walk. As I stand in the water it feels cool and refreshing against my skin. I feel the warm sun beating against my shoulders and the gentle breeze blows from time to time. I hear the waves crashing against the shore. There are also seagulls off in the distance squawking. I also taste salt on my lips from swimming in the ocean water.

WRITE YOUR "HAPPY PLACE" DESCRIPTION.

_____

_____

_____

_____

_____

_____

_____

_____

_____

_____

_____

_____

_____

_____

_____

_____

_____

Draw your "happy place."

What's On Your Plate?

Objective: For girls to learn how to manage stress by adopting a lifestyle with good balance.

Information: Stress is inevitable. We all have stress in our lives. A lot of stress has to do with responsibilities and events that others our age are going through too such as tests, homework, or performing in a school play or sporting event. Sometimes individuals can be stressed by overcommitting to extracurricular activities. It's important to monitor all of your commitments to make sure that you get enough time to rest and re-energize.

Procedure: Have group members write down all of their responsibilities and commitments that require their time on their plates. Have the girls discuss all of the stressors that can be eliminated from their lives and have them write down coping skills to manage the stressors. For example, someone might eliminate an activity such as "Drama Club" because their packed schedule is adding to their high stress levels. If math class is causing a high level of stress it needs to be addressed.

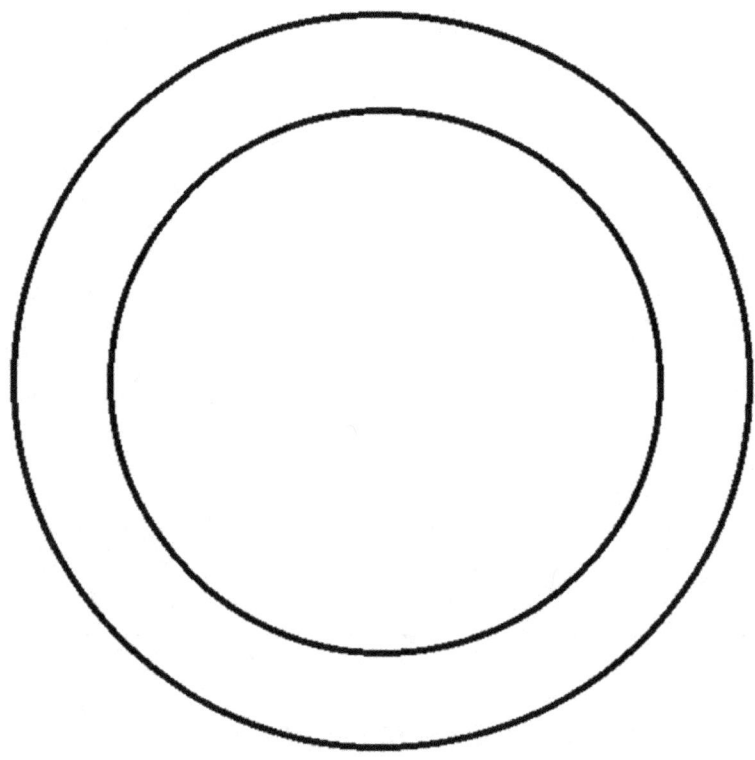

Coping Skills

1.
2.
3.
4.
5.

Discussion Questions

1. What are some physical signs or symptoms that you experience when you are feeling a high level of stress? (headaches, stomach aches, feeling tired etc..)
2. What are some mental signs or symptoms that you experience when you are feeling a high level of stress? (Feeling frustrated or anxious, negative thoughts, difficulty concentrating)
3. What are some behaviors that you engage in when you are feeling stressed out? (Yelling at someone, sleeping more or less, crying)
4. What are some coping skills you use to help you relax when you are feeling stressed out?
5. Do you have any unhealthy coping skills? (Sleeping excessively, isolating yourself, self-injury?) If so, come up with a list of positive coping skills to substitute the negative coping skills.

Ignore, Distract, or Address

Objective: For girls to learn how to handle different types of problems.

Procedure: We encounter numerous amounts of stressors on a regular basis. It is important to recognize how different events and situations affect us and the best way to respond. Have group members write three examples of problems/stressors where they should use each strategy.

Let it go? Ask yourself the following questions. Is it a huge deal? Will it bother you for an hour, a week, longer? Is there an easy or quick solution? Sometimes it's not worth holding on to a stressor if it will only cause us to remain angry.

Distract yourself? Is it a problem that doesn't have a quick solution? Sometimes you might need to time to process how to solve a problem. However, it could be helpful to give your mind a break and come back to the problem later with a fresh perspective.

Address It: Have you processed your decision? Thought about the consequences? Sometimes addressing the problem is difficult or uncomfortable, but the long-term results are for the best.

I will let these stressors go:

-
-
-
-
-

I will use distraction with these stressors:

-
-
-
-
-

I will address the following stressors/problems:

-
-
-
-
-

STAYING HEALTHY

Objective: For girls to learn how to adopt a healthy lifestyle by tending to their mental and physical well-being.

Procedure: Life can be really busy and stressful. It's important that we take care of ourselves in order to take on daily challenges. What are things that you can do on a daily basis to take care of your physical and mental health? Have your group keep a journal log to keep track of mental/physical health activities that they are doing on a regular basis. Have girls reflect on their week and make changes if they need to improve in any areas. Encourage girls to add items to the activities lists as well.

Mental Health Activities	**Physical Health Activities**
Deep Breathing	Eat Healthy
Quiet Time	Drink Water
Reading	Exercise
Going Outside	Walk Your Dog
Bubble Bath	Limit Sugar Intake
Listen to music	Get Enough Sleep
Spend time with family or friends	Washing your hands

Sun	Mon	Tues	Wed	Thurs	Fri	Sat
P:	P:	P:	P:	P:	P:	P:
M:	M:	M:	M:	M:	M:	M:

Discussion Questions

1. What do you think of when it comes to "physical health?"
2. What do you think of when it comes to "mental health?"
3. When it comes to physical health what is one thing in which you are doing well? What is what thing you would like to improve?
4. When it comes to mental health what is one thing in which you are doing well? What is one thing you would like to improve?
5. How can taking care of your mental health be just as important as taking care of your physical health?
6. How are establishing healthy routines helpful?
7. What are different activities that you can practice at school?
8. What are activities that you can do at home?
9. Think back to the last time you felt stressed out. Were there certain activities that could have helped you feel better?
10. What are other some other activities that you find helpful that can be added to the list?

Distractions to Obtain Calm

Objective: For girls to identify different distraction techniques that they can implement to overcome intense feelings such as anxiety.

Procedure: It's important for individuals to recognize when their emotions are starting to escalate in order to pick an intervention strategy. This is an important skill to prevent panic attacks from occurring. Encourage group members to go over the list of distraction activities that can be implemented in order to distract themselves when thoughts of worry are taking over. Afterwards, have the girls write down exercises that they can practice in different settings. Group members are encouraged to come up with their own ideas as well.

- Focus on something or someone for a couple minutes and make observations.

- Pick a color and look around you to count how many places you see that color.

- Listen to a song and how focus on how the beat feels.

- Write down a top ten list of your favorite things such as animals, sports, hobbies, colors, food etc...

- Write down the United States in Alphabetical Order

- Write down as many European and African countries that you can recall.

- Look out the window and count and observe the things that move by.

- Watch the clouds in the sky and notice their shapes and movements.

- Doodle on a piece of paper without putting any thought into what you will draw.

What are three exercises that I can do at school?

    1.

    2.

    3.

What are three exercises that I can do at home?

    1.

    2.

    3.

What are three exercises that I can do in public?

    1.

    2.

    3.

Discussion Questions

1. 1. What are some physical signs that you are getting worried/anxious?
2. 2. What thoughts run through your mind when you get nervous?
3. 3. What are some situations where distraction can be helpful?
4. 4. Share a time when you felt your anxiety rising at school?
5. 5. Which distraction exercises do you like the most? Why?

COPING SKILLS CHART

Objective: For girls to learn different coping skills to use

Procedure: Have group members look at the chart and pick strategies that they could use. Afterwards, go over discussion questions.

Positive Life Choices	Contemplation	Distraction	Focus on others	Use support system
Practice positive self-talk	Keep a journal to track your goals	Listen to music	Volunteer	Identify people you can count on
Have a good attitude	Forgive yourself for past mistakes	Watch a funny movie clip	Do something to show you care about someone	Make a list of five people who you can reach out to when needed
Practice having an optimistic outlook	Practice deep breathing	Go for a run/workout	Be open-minded to new situations and people	Practice how you can go about asking for help
Remain drug/alcohol free	Visualize something peaceful	Play with your pet	Reach out to someone new	Identify times when it's necessary to ask for help
Make responsible choices	Take pictures of people and things that make you happy. Keep one with you	Do something fun. (Take a walk in a park or go to the movies)	Join a sport, club, or activity at your school or in your community	Spend quality time with your family
Have the ability to move forward vs. dwelling on the past	Recognize when your emotions are escalating	Use a stress ball	Teach something to a younger sibling or friend	Identify a positive role model in your life

Celebrate your success (big or small)	Taking a break from an argument to calm down	Spend time drawing or painting	Offer support to a peer in need	Ask someone about how they have overcome personal obstacles
Establish good balance with responsibilities and "me time"	Think about how you set your priorities and make changes if necessary	Try baking or cooking a tasty treat	Pick a charity and help their cause	Schedule time in your day to talk to a family member or friend about the high point and low point of your day
Accept changes and stay flexible	Keep a gratitude journal. Every day write down something you are grateful for	Try a new hobby	Thank someone who has helped you	Keep individuals in your support system updated about your goals
Make decisions to demonstrate respecting yourself	How are your sleep patterns? Adopt a good sleep schedule if needed	Clean out your closets and donate your old clothes	Perform a random act of kindness for someone	Make the effort to get to know one of your teachers or coaches
Make a schedule to stay organized	Focus on tightening and relaxing your muscles. Try to identify when you are feeling tense	Learn something new (a card trick or how to knit)	Help someone reach one of their goals	Catch up with a friend who you haven't seen in a while

DISCUSSION QUESTIONS

1. How do you think each of these categories could be important when overcoming stressful situations?
2. Which coping strategies could you do at school?
3. Which coping strategies would you choose to use at home or in public?
4. Which coping strategies do you think would be the most helpful for you? Why?
5. Which coping strategies would be the most difficult for you to implement? Why?
6. When do you see yourself using these coping strategies?
7. Can you think of other ideas to add to this list?

SELF ESTEEM

Celebrate Being Me!

Objective: For girls to appreciate their unique qualities that make up their amazing selves.

Procedure: Have group members write down the following prompts and then have them take turns sharing their responses with each other.

I believe……

What makes me unique is…

My favorite quote is…

What makes me happy when I'm feeling down is…

What matters most to me is…

I hope to see this change in the world…

I wish…

One day I will…

One of my strengths is…

All of My Strengths

Objective: To teach girls the importance in focusing on positive personal attributes as opposed to only viewing negative attributes.

Information: It can be difficult for individuals to identify and appreciate personal strengths. It seems easier to identify our flaws and negative comments that someone might say about us. Although it is important to be aware of weaknesses in order to set goals, it is essential that individuals learn to love and accept themselves for who they are!

Procedure: Have group members fill out the following worksheet. They will start out by filling out their strengths or areas where they feel confident. Discuss the importance in recognizing positive characteristics. Afterwards, have girls fill out the section about their insecurities. However, they will have to think of how they can change their insecurities into a positive attribute.

Strengths

My personality or who I am as a person

-
-
-
-
-
-

My abilities or what I do well

-
-
-
-
-
-

My goals for the future

-
-
-
-
-
-

Insecurities About Myself

-
-
-
-
-

How can I view my insecurities differently? What positives have resulted from your insecurity?

Example: Personality

- I am really quiet and wish I was more outgoing.
- Being quiet has allowed me to become a good listener.

Example: Abilities

- Math is really difficult for me.
- Although I don't do well on math tests I show teachers I'm a good student by always completing my homework.

Example: Appearance

- I feel insecure about how tall I am.
- My height is an asset in the sports I play.

Insecurities

My personality or who I am as a person

-

-

My abilities or what I do well.

-

-

My appearance or the way I look.

-

-

Discussion Questions

1. What do you think are factors that contribute to building self-confidence?
2. What do you think are obstacles to building self-confidence?
3. Why do you think it's important to attempt to view your insecurities in a more positive way?
4. Was it easier to point out your strengths or insecurities? Why?
5. What are things you can do to help remind yourself to reframe your insecurities into strengths?

Build Her Up

Objective: Improve self-esteem and teach girls to identify positive characteristics in others.

Procedure: This activity could be done in one session or every girl can get a chance to participate at the beginning of different sessions. It is suggested to do this activity once the girls in the group have gotten to know each other.

1. Have girls write down 5 things that they like or appreciate about the girl who will be "built up" on cards.
2. Encourage them to take their time and come up with genuine and thoughtful statements.
3. Girls will go around in a circle taking turns sharing one compliment at a time.
4. Afterwards, the girl who was built up can put her cards in a place that will remind her of the positive characteristics that she has. A good place to post the cards might be in a locker, journal, or mirror.

Follow-Up Questions

1. How did it feel to be the girl who was receiving the positive statements and compliments?
2. Is it easier to focus on positive characteristics about yourself or others? Why?
3. Why do you think some girls tend to point out other girls' negative characteristics easily?
4. What are your favorite types of compliments to receive?
5. What do you think the world would be like if we made it a common practice to build people up?

STAYING POSITIVE

Objective: For girls to learn to identify positive statements and events in order to practice positive self-talk.

Information: Why is it sometimes easier to remember all the mean or hurtful things that people say to us, but it is difficult to remember all of the positive statements people say to us or all of our accomplishments? It is important for everyone to practice holding onto the positives in order to help our emotional selves grow.

Procedure: Have group members fill out a positive memories in each of the flower's petals. It could be a compliment received, a personal strength or accomplishment, or a happy memory. Group members will write out negative thoughts or statements that have caused hurt or negative feelings. Afterwards, the group will share what they have written in their petals and rain drops. Group members can color in or decorate their flowers and rip up and throw away rain drops at the end of the group.

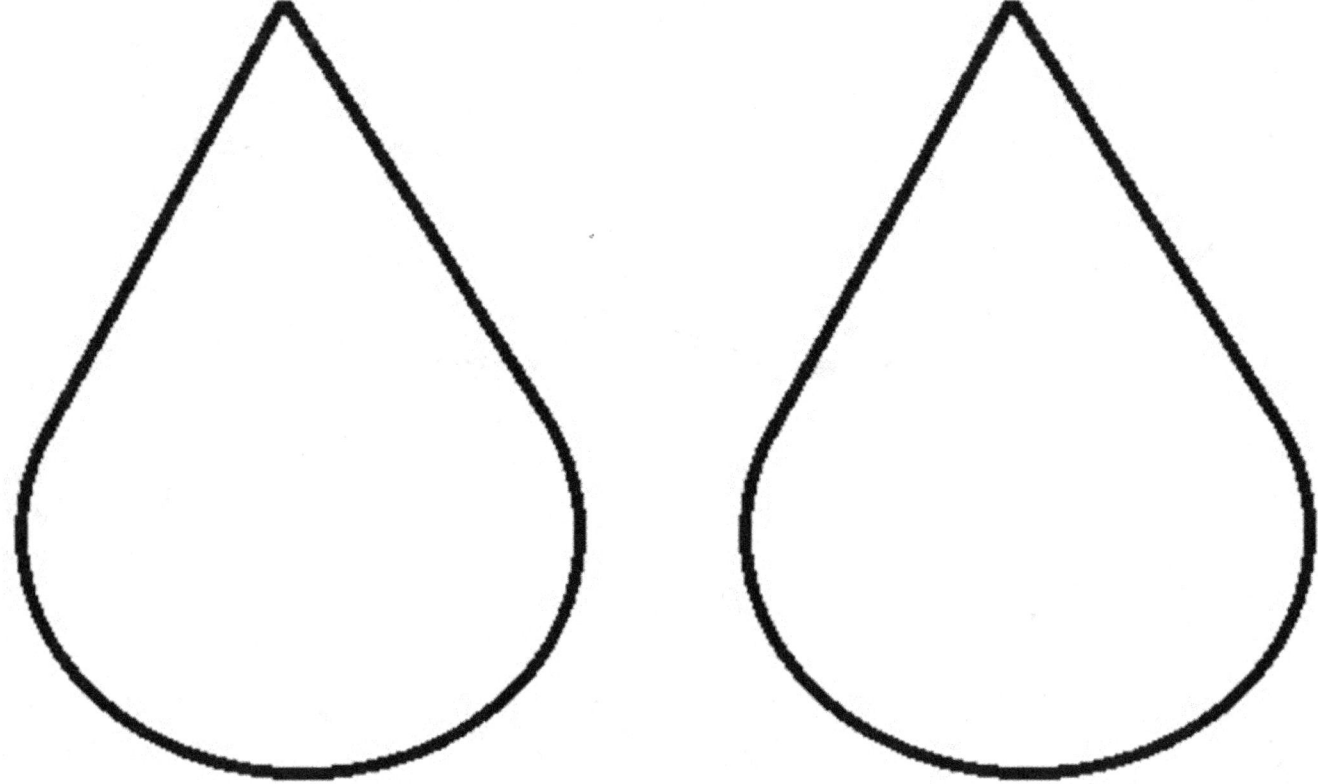

I Accept Me

Objective: For girls to learn to accept and celebrate their unique qualities that make them one of a kind.

Materials: magazines, scissors, canvas or paper, paste

Procedure: Have girls search for words and pictures in magazines or printouts from the internet that describe themselves. Once girls are done cutting out their images they can use paste to put together a collage that they can keep in a safe place. Afterwards, the group will answer the following questions.

One thing that I do well is:

The part of my personality that I love most is:

I would never change this about myself:

Select a mantra to include in your collage. Feel free to write your own as well.

I love the person I am.

I appreciate both my strengths and accept my weaknesses.

I am going to be the best me I can be.

There is only one me in the world.

Embracing Me

Objective: For girls to reflect on times where they made a positive difference in their lives.

Procedure: At times it can be difficult to name personal strengths, but breaking it down into different categories and memories allows individuals to reflect on their past and to feel good about themselves and their actions. Have group members fill in the following statements.

One time I helped someone:

One time I got a good grade after studying:

One time I made a responsible decision:

One time I showed self-discipline:

One time I showed kindness to someone in need:

One time I overcame an obstacle:

One time I controlled my temper when I was mad:

One time I stood up for something I believe in:

One time I created something which made me proud:

One time I volunteered:

One time I didn't give into peer pressure:

One time I accepted a compliment wholeheartedly:

One time I overcame a fear:

My Bucket List

———

Objective: For girls to identify goals they wish to accomplish and situations they wish to experience.

Procedure: Have group members write a list of things they want to do, see, or accomplish in their lifetimes.

1   6.   11.

2.   7.   12.

3.   8.   13.

4.   9.   14.

5.   10.   15.

D ISCUSSION Q UESTION

1. Was it difficult or easy to think of your bucket list items?
2. How do your items reflect who you are as a person?
3. Have you set a plan to accomplish any items yet?
4. Are there items that you think will take a long time to complete? Why?
5. Why are bucket lists important?
6. Do you think your bucket list will change as you get older? Why/why not?
7. How could just thinking about your bucket list be helpful in stressful situations?
8. Did other group members have any similar items on their bucket lists?
9. Have you already completed a bucket list items?
10. After hearing other group members' bucket lists, did you add any to your own list?

Letter to my Past and Future Self

Objective: For girls to reflect on areas of growth that they have accomplished as well as to identify goals and changes they would like to make in the future.

Procedure: Have girls write a letter to themselves from a time period in the past. Have them write a letter to their future selves as well. They are allowed to choose how many years into the past or future they would like to write to themselves. The following list of questions could be used to prompt some writing responses for girls to include in their letters.

Letter to Past Self

- The best thing occurring in your life at the time
- The most challenging thing occurring in your life at the time
- Advice you would give yourself if you could do something differently
- One area in which you have grown
- Express compassion to your past self

Letter to Future Self

- How do you envision yourself? What is one thing you'll still want to be doing and what is something that you hope that is different?
- What do you anticipate being the most challenging obstacle in your life?
- What is an area you hope to improve upon?
- Who are people you still hope to have in your life?
- What is one hope you have for your future self?

DISCUSSION QUESTIONS

1. What was this experience like for you to write to yourself in the past and future?
2. What was the most challenging part of this exercise for you?
3. How did you select the timeframe to write to your past self? What was going on in your life at that time?
4. When do you plan to read your letter to your future self?